Curious · Little · Catholic · Series

What is a Vocation?

Annemarie **Thimons**

Illustrated by
Nancy Rosato–Nuzzo

What is a Vocation?
Curious Little Catholic Series
Annemarie Thimons

Illustrated by Nancy Rosato–Nuzzo

Copyright © 2020, Annemarie Thimons. All rights reserved.

No part of this book may be reproduced, stored in a retrieval system or transmitted in any form or by any means - electronic, mechanical, photocopying, recording, or otherwise - without written permission of the author.

For additional inspirational books visit us at CuriousLittleCatholic.com

Author's Note:

There are many facets of our Catholic faith that are difficult for pre-schoolers to understand. These books have been written as enrichment for the littlest, yet curious, young Catholic children. Should you desire, the scripture verses accompanying each page can be easily memorized by young children. We hope the memorization of these key verses will help strengthen the child's foundation when later studying apologetics. We hope these books will be a beautiful addition to the bookshelves of families who are striving to build homes that foster vocations.

Totus Tuus!

What is a Vocation?

**A Vocation is your life work.
It is a beautiful calling
that God has just for you.**

*"He has saved us and called us to a holy life,
not according to our works but according to his own design
and the grace bestowed on us in Christ Jesus before time began."
2 Timothy 1:9*

A vocation is the path that leads our soul to heaven. It is a very important and precious thing.

"My soul proclaims the greatness of the Lord; my spirit rejoices in God my Savior."
Luke 1:46

Each of us has a calling to motherhood or fatherhood.

"Your wife will be like a fruitful vine within your home, your children like young olive plants around your table."
Psalm 128:3

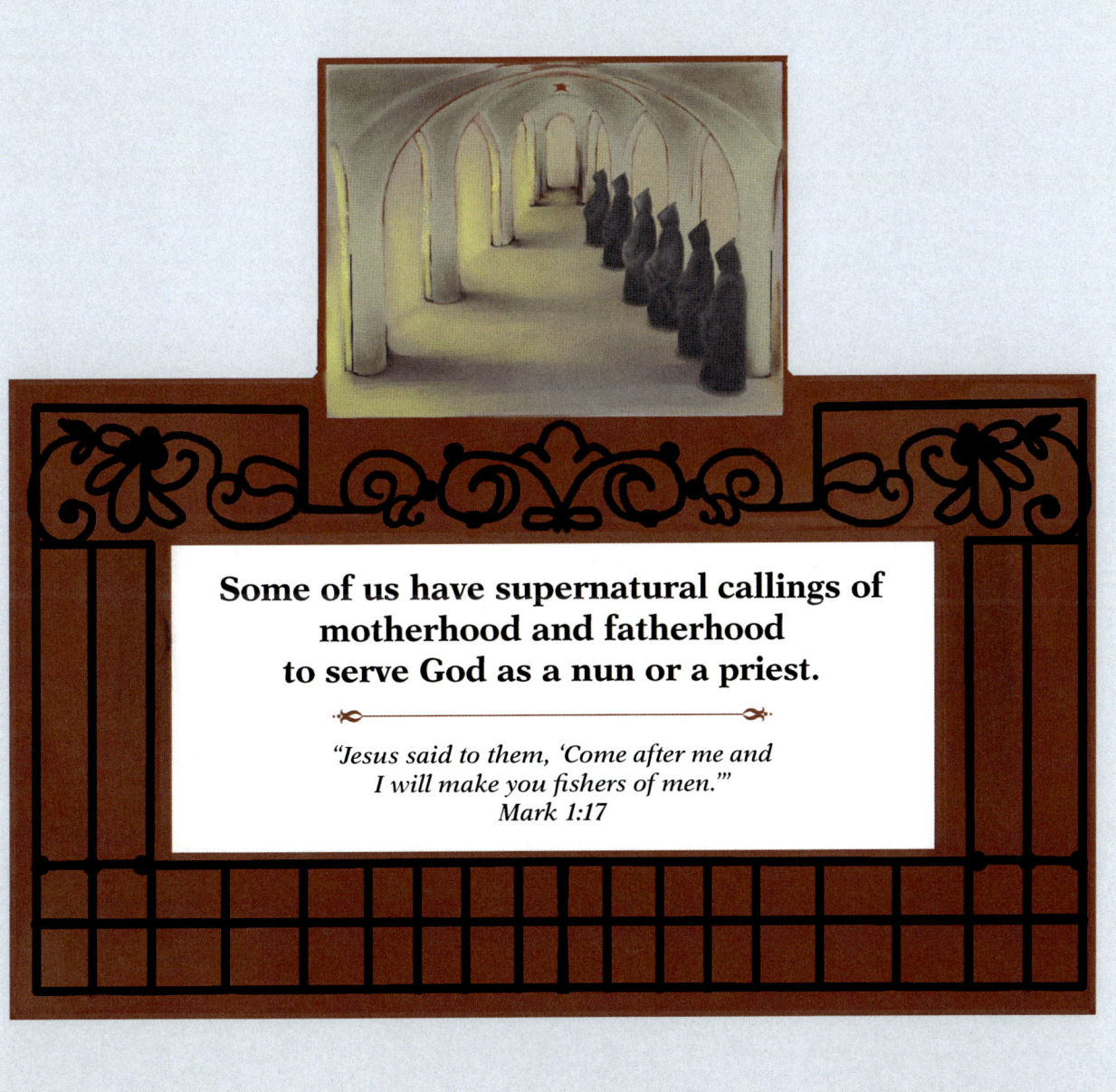

Some of us have supernatural callings of motherhood and fatherhood to serve God as a nun or a priest.

"Jesus said to them, 'Come after me and I will make you fishers of men.'"
Mark 1:17

Everyone is called to love God above all and to do our best to love others.

"Amen, amen I say to you whatever you did for one of these least brothers of mine, you did for me."
Matthew 25:40

We are all called to use our life work for the greater glory of God, that is, to do all that we do for Him.

⦁――◆――⦁

"And all day long, both at the temple and in their homes they did not stop teaching and proclaiming the Messiah, Jesus."
Acts 5:42

In every choice we make, we ask ourselves "Is this bringing me closer to heaven or farther away?" We want to make choices that bring us closer to heaven, like climbing a little ladder towards God.

"Proclaim the word, be persistent whether it is convenient or inconvenient."
2 Timothy 4:2

How do we know what our vocation is? We have to pray and we have to spend time being with Our Lord.

"Make known to me your ways, Lord; teach me your path."
Psalm 25:4

**Sometimes it takes a long time to find out.
Sometimes we know right away!**

*"Discern what is of value, so that you may be pure and blameless
for the day of Christ."
Philippians 1:10*

You will know what your vocation is when you feel peace which leads to great joy in your heart.

"Mary said, 'Behold I am the handmaid of the Lord. May it be done unto me according to thy word.'"
Luke 1:38

**Finding your vocation
is a very beautiful thing.
It is our whole purpose for why God made us.**

*"So whether you eat or drink,
or whatever you do, do everything for the glory of God."
1 Corinthians 10:31*

Before you go to sleep each night, ask your angel to protect your special vocation, whatever it may be and thank God for the beautiful gift he has given just to you.

"In all circumstances, hold faith as a shield, to quench all flaming arrows of the evil one. And take the helmet of salvation and the sword of the spirit which is the word of God."
Ephesians 6:16-17

Orders Featured

Page 4 **Franciscan Sisters of the Eucharist**
405 Allen Avenue
Meriden, CT 06451
(203) 238–2243
www.franciscansistersoftheeucharist.org

Page 6 **Sisters of Bethlehem**
Monastery of Our Lady in Beatitude
393 Our Lady of Lourdes Road
Livingston Manor, NY 12758
(845) 439–4300

Page 8 **Benedictine Monks**
Monastero di San Benedetto
Via Reguardati 22
06046 Norcia (PG) Italy
(39) 0743-817125
(39) 0743-828425
www.osbnorcia.org

Page 10 **Capuchin Franciscans**
www.capuchin.org

Page 11 **Sister Adorers of the Royal Heart of Jesus Christ Sovereign Priest**
Institute of Christ the King
6415 S. Woodlawn Avenue
Chicago, Illinois 60637-3817
(773) 363–7409
www.institute-christ-king.org/vocations/sisters/

Page 12 **The Marians of the Immaculate Conception of the Blessed Virgin Mary**
Eden Hill
Stockbridge, MA 01263
(413) 298–3931
www.marian.org

Page 16 **Holy Spirit Sisters of Adoration**
2212 Green Street
Philadelphia, PA 19130
(215) 567–0123
www.adorationsisters.org

Page 18 **Dominican Sisters of Mary, Mother of the Eucharist**
4597 Warren Road
Ann Arbor, MI 48105
(734) 994–7437
www.sistersofmary.org

Page 19 **Sisters of Life**
38 Montebello Road
Suffern, NY 10901
(845) 357–3547
www.sistersoflife.org

Page 21 **Handmaids of the Precious Blood For Christ in His Priest**
Cor Jesu Monastery
596 Callaway Ridge
New Market, TN 37820
www.nunsforpriests.org

About the Author:

Annemarie (Nuzzo) Thimons is a graduate of Mother of Divine Grace Homestudy and Franciscan University of Steubenville. The Curious Catholic Series was inspired by her five children, whom she and her husband Tom homeschool in New York. She is blessed to have her mother, Nancy, illustrating the stories. She would love to hear stories of sharing the Curious Little Catholic series in your home: www.curiouslittlecatholic.com

About the Illustrator:

Nancy Rosato-Nuzzo, is a freelance illustrator currently working in the beautiful Hudson Valley, New York. A graduate of Long Island University School of the Arts, she is a mixed-media artist who is inspired by the divinity she sees concealed within the daily cadence of life. When she is not in her studio, this mother of three, grandmother of 9, enjoys cooking, gardening, and listening to the music of her husband of 36 years. She is delighted to be collaborating with her daughter on this project.